SUPERNATURA
SOUL - STIRRING TESTIMONY

For the Glory of God and Salvation of Lost Souls

DOES-GOD-STILL PERFORM MIRACLES TODAY?

TOMMY THOMAS' LIFE STORY

The man who spent years behind prison bars —on chain-gangs and in stockades down south—was a dope-fiend, drunkard, pick-pocket, short-changer, confidence man and counterfeiter. Spent years in carnival life. His body was healed from heart trouble, dropsy, pellagra, the first stage of cancer and other diseases—All
THROUGH FAITH IN GOD

Known as "Believing Thomas"
A Mystery to the World and a Puzzle to the Devil

Impression as Tommy looked before his conversion. This same boy was once the idol of his dead mother's heart. Dabbling in sin led to it all. Only God's mercy spared him for a pattern to warn young boys and girls not to undertake, but to give their hearts to Jesus while young and tender—that they escape the horrors of dabbling in sin and finally lose their souls and their reward without Jesus in a lake of God's boiling wrath of fire and brimstone forever and ever.

Federal Bureau of Investigation
United States Department of Justice
Washington, D. C.

The following is the record of FBI number 820164

J. E. Hoover
Director

This record, from Washington, D. C., from J. Edgar Hoover's office, the head of the F.B.I., shows Tommy's records, what sin leads to. This only shows where he was picked up and finger printed. Also his record when he did time in two Federal prisons, Atlanta, Ga., and Leavenworth, Kans. He has done much time on chain gangs and stockades that is not on record. Sin caused it all. Look this record over closely.

This is more of Tommy's record from the head of the F.B.I., J. Edgar Hoover's office, Washington, D. C. Check this record closely. These records are taken from the original, to smaller cuts for book use. Anyone doubting these records, call or wire J. Edgar Hoover, the head of the F.B.I., Washington, D. C.

As Believing Thomas looks today while this book is being printed—and the blood of Jesus Christ cleansed from all sin and sanctified him wholly by the Holy Ghost. He is now telling to all the world of lost sinners there is all power in the Blood of Jesus and supernatural power in Second Blessing Holiness.

Rev. Howard Hughes of 896 North Main St., Marion, Ohio, the man who led Tommy Thomas to the Stranger of Galilee, Jesus, on Christmas Day, 1942, in the Marion County jail. What a Christmas gift Tommy received. Give God the glory.

Rev. Wm. R. Hannan, Pilgrim Holiness evan-
gelist of 658 West Jefferson St., Springfield,
Ohio. This man of God was very helpful in
getting Tommy Thomas established in Second
Blessing Holiness. Give God the glory.

FOREWORD

This book, by the help of the Holy Spirit, was written by Tommy Thomas. Mrs. Florence Witte gave much of her time in preparing the manuscript.

I was asked the other day, "Will the book of Tommy Thomas be printed the way he preaches, or will you change it to conform with English composition?" I immediately replied, "If I changed his book, it would not read as Tommy Thomas preaches."

I would to God there were more men who could visualize the winning of souls as Brother Thomas does. *"He that winneth souls is wise."*—Prov. 11:30.

This soul-stirring testimony will capture you in such a way as to make you think of what you are now doing and of where you will spend eternity.

The book is being sent forth on the wings of prayer. May it be a blessing to the readers, as it has been to me in preparing it for publication.

May God's richest blessing, that maketh rich and addeth no sorrow, rest upon the efforts put forth, is my prayer.

P. Lewis Brevard

CONTENTS

INTRODUCTION

I have always believed the greatest power of the church is the personal testimony.

This little book by "Believing Thomas" ought to seal the mouths of those who say that people don't want God. There are hungry hearts everywhere, and even those who are looked upon as great sinners hunger after God. Some have questioned the advisability of a man's telling of his past life, but anyone hearing or reading this marvelous testimony of Brother Thomas ought to be convinced that Jesus is able to save to the uttermost all those that come unto God by Him.

It ought to put many of us to shame to see to what extreme the devil's devotees will go, and what power he has over them to drive them to madness to accomplish his purpose. This testimony shows the great transforming power of God, what He can do in so marvelously changing a man and making him as zealous in telling the story of Jesus and working for the Master as he was in serving the devil.

We believe the secret of Brother Thomas' victorious life is that he not only was born of the Spirit, but he went on and received the blessing of Entire Sanctification which made him more than conqueror through Him that loved him.

We pray that God's blessing will continue to be upon him and the work he is doing for the lost, and that this little book will be instrumental in winning many to the Christ-of-God.

Meredith G. Standley

LIFE STORY OF TOMMY THOMAS

To warn a younger generation not to undertake to follow my footsteps and fall into this terrible pit.

HOW CAN YOU ESCAPE?

Give your heart to God when you are young and tender.

I am giving only the high points of the story of my life's history, as I would not undertake to tell all the little things that I have done while in sin and of the many 30, 60, and 90 days I have done time in jails, on chain gangs and stockades in the southlands.

1 Timothy 1:15, 16.

This is a faithful saying, and worthy of all acceptation, that Christ Jesus came into the world to save sinners of whom I am chief. Howbeit for this cause I obtained mercy, that in me first Jesus Christ might shew forth all longsuffering, for a pattern to them which should hereafter believe on Him to Life Everlasting.

Born in Putnam County, Cookeville, Tennessee, reared in Bloody Mingo County, Williamson, West Virginia; county of the Hatfield McCoy feud, in the hills of West Virginia, known as

BELIEVING THOMAS

Hobby words, "Ain't I a sight on the devil and his works."

CHAPTER I

*Called of God from prison cell to pulpit to expound
the power of the blood of Jesus Christ and to
warn and to show this younger generation
and the world the only sure escape
from sin and hell.*

The early days of my life I lived in Putnam County, Tennessee, known as Bloody Eight, Silver Point, until I was eight years old. My daddy and my mother were both school teachers, but sin was in the home. I had only one brother. When I was eight years of age, our family moved to Bloody County, Mingo, West Virginia, and my father became a railroad worker. My mother began to be afflicted with poor health, and died and left me when I was but twelve years of age. My father, I am sorry to say, was like many of the fathers of boys and girls of this generation, and would drink and carouse around with other women. My brother and I were turned out to do the best we knew how. At last my father had a nervous breakdown from drinking and impaired health, and was also afflicted with T. B. The doctors gave him an insanity test and sent him to the Spencer West Virginia Insane State Hospital, at which place he died later on. He was dead and buried seven months before I knew of it. My father's death came around the age of 29. My brother and I were now out in the world trying to do the best we could, with no home, no God, no father, no mother, no Sunday School—forsaken by all except JESUS.

15

CHAPTER II

All of my people dead.

Here are some things that sin leads to.

As far as I know at this time I had no relatives left on either my father's or my mother's side, not even a grandfather or grandmother, with the ex-. ception of two first cousins who now live in Tennessee. Some of my kin folks had made whiskey, and some of them died that I knew nothing about. One uncle was found dead in bed, and an aunt was found dead also from drinking. One uncle was found in the road with his head cut off. My two cousins are without God now, as far as I know, but I am praying for them.

CHAPTER III

What dabbling in sin will lead to.

You do not know what you will do when the devil gets you wrapped up in his power. Did you know, dear reader, that every man and woman, boy and girl in reformatories, penitentiaries, chain gangs, asylums, hell holes, boweries, and all those who are walking the corridors of these places were once the idols of mothers' hearts? Some of the devil's devices that he uses in getting this younger generation, mothers and fathers are dabbling in playing cards for fun, bingo parties, bowling alleys, roller rinks, beaches, parties, shows, circuses, county fairs, carnivals, parks and such like. Many people think and say, and many modern preachers say there is no harm in this and that dabbling. These are all of the devil as I know about all these things myself especially carnival life, shows, and county fairs as I was right in the carnival world myself. I happen to know what these devices and snares of the devil will lead to. Ephesians 6:10, 11, 12. "Finally, my brethren, be strong in the Lord, and in the power of His might. PUT ON THE WHOLE ARMOUR OF GOD, THAT YE MAY BE ABLE TO STAND AGAINST THE WILES (OR SNARES AND TRICKS) OF THE DEVIL. For we wrestle not against flesh and blood, but against principalities, against powers, against the RULERS OF THE DARKNESS OF THIS WORLD,

AGAINST SPIRITUAL WICKEDNESS IN HIGH PLACES."

Dear reader, do not misunderstand me. I am not trying to club or skin you, nor hurt you, but if you are a sinner and do these things, you cannot help yourself and you have all the devil has got, but thank God, there is hope for you. Let Jesus do unto you as He has done unto me and to others who were bound by the chains of Satan, and let Him save your soul and clean your heart. Isaiah 1:18. "Come now, and let us reason together, saith the Lord: though your sins be as scarlet, they shall be as white as snow; though they be red like crimson, they shall be as wool." There is power in the Blood of Jesus. I John 1:7. "But if we walk in the light, as He is in the light, we have fellowship one with another, and the **BLOOD OF JESUS CHRIST HIS SON CLEANSETH** us from ALL sin." John 3:16 says, "For God so loved the world, that He gave His only begotten Son, that **WHOSOEVER** believeth in Him should not perish, but have **EVERLASTING LIFE.**" Revelation 22:17 says "And the Spirit and the Bride say Come. And let him that heareth say, Come. And let him that is athirst, Come, and **WHOSOEVER WILL** let him take the water of LIFE freely." **WHOSOEVER WILL** means YOU, dear reader who is without God. If you turn from sin and accept the provision for your salvation under the Blood of Christ, you will never be sorry in this world or in the world to come.

CHAPTER IV

Setting up kitty cats at carnivals.

*At the beginning of my dabbling in sin.
Although we are all born with sin in
our heart, Jesus is the remedy.*

Now get this, sinner (if you be one). When I
was fourteen years of age, living in Bloody Mingo
County, Williamson, West Virginia, a carnival came
to town, and I went over and got a job setting up
Kitty Cats on this traveling paraphernalia of the
devil that leads people to hell. I thought, "O
there is no harm in setting up Kitty Cats," but dear
reader, this is just what the devil wants to do with
his sly tricks and wiles—get a hook in the jaw of
this younger generation. Mothers, fathers, young
and old all get their eyes upon his devilish devices
of sin and filth which turns mother and father and
that pure boy and virgin girl morally to become
a thief, a robber, a murderer, a drinker, an adulterer,
a liar, a beggar, a dope fiend, a marihuanna fiend;
and eventually burn in that lake of fire which is
hell. Revelation 21:8 "But the fearful, and unbe-
lieving, and the abominable, and murderers, and
whoremongers, and sorcerers, and idolaters, and all
liars, shall have their part in the lake which burn-
eth with fire and brimstone; which is the second
death."

My God, my God, please dear people as you read

this book, let God speak to your hearts, and I pray that you will flee from such trash of the devil and the world. Please come to Jesus who can give you something lasting. He can give you peace, joy, happiness, and health and above what the human mind can imagine. Matthew 11:28, "Come unto me, all ye that labor and are heavy laden, and I WILL GIVE YOU REST. Take my yoke upon you, and learn of me; for I am meek and lowly in heart: and ye SHALL FIND REST UNTO YOUR SOULS. For my yoke is easy, and my burden is light." John 16:24, "Hitherto have ye asked nothing in my name: ASK, AND YE SHALL RECEIVE, THAT YOUR JOY MAY BE FULL." Ephesians 3:20, "Now unto Him that is able to do exceeding abundantly above all that we ask or think, according to the power that worketh in us." Oh, if you be a sinner, as you read these few words, think about your soul. Just give Jesus one chance. This plea is from a man who has been down to the depths of hell, but oh, one touch of the sacred hand of God, and He brought deliverance—broke every fetter, and brought peace to his soul and heart that the world and carnival life, night clubs, and the gay lights of New York and Philadelphia and St. Louis, the boweries, hell holes, and taverns could not give.

After staying in the carnival life with the devil's gang for six years, I became a drunkard, gambler, short changer, pick pocket, confidence man, dope fiend; also began serving much time in jails, stockades and chain gangs. On and on I went on this downward road in sin and saw and felt the horrors of what sin will lead to behind prison bars, and

some of the devil's underworld. I was once thus
deep in sin and ready to drop into hell, but the
Stranger of Galilee had His hand on me. It seems
that all this has been permitted for a purpose and
a pattern to show this world that there is Power
in the Blood of Jesus to save to the uttermost.
Hebrews 7:25, "Wherefore He is able also to save
them to the uttermost that come unto God by him,
seeing He ever liveth to make intercession for them."

Oh, dear reader, if you be a sinner, do not, I beg
of you, fall into sin as I did. The only way of escape is Jesus. John 14:6, "Jesus saith unto him,
I AM THE WAY, THE TRUTH, AND THE
LIFE; no man cometh unto the Father, but by
ME." The Word of God says, "And be sure your
sin will find you out."—Numbers 32:23.

May this supernatural, dynamic testimony stir
your soul and heart and cause you to turn (if you
be in sin) from sin and darkness to light and glory,
which is Jesus. John 8:12, "Then spake Jesus again
unto them, saying, I AM THE LIGHT OF THE
WORLD: he that followeth ME shall not walk in
darkness, but shall have the LIGHT OF LIFE."

Dear reader, if you be a mother, or a father,
young boy or young girl, perhaps you say in your
heart that you would not do what Tommy Thomas
has done, (if you be a sinner) by dabbling in sin
and countless multitudes have said the same thing.
Those same folks who have said they would not do
such things are now walking the corridors of yonder
Hell. I know that WHOSOEVER will let Jesus
come into their life NOW, they will never do these
things. II Peter 1:10 says, "Wherefore the rather,

brethren, give diligence to make your calling and election sure; for if YE DO THESE THINGS YE SHALL NEVER FALL." Please heed my warning, and this is a plea from a man who loves God and lost souls that do not know Jesus.

CHAPTER V

Diseases begin to creep in on my body.

God tried to stop me on this downward plunge to Hell.

After all these years of serving the devil and his following, at the age of about twenty-eight my heart began to flutter, this affliction being pronounced by doctors to be an alcoholic, enlarged, fluttering heart. My ankles swelled up with dropsy, and also pellagra crept in for which there is no cure outside of a miracle through the touch of God. This condition may be described as the red corpuscles in the blood eating up the white corpuscles. I also had the first stage of cancer from drink, as I had been drinking bay rum, rubbing alcohol, canned heat, and hair tonic. God permitted all this to come upon me in order that He might stop me long enough to talk to my conscience about my lost soul. I was just like most all of the world of sinners who the devil has deceived, and wait until the last minute on a death bed to repent.

I was in St. Francis Hospital in Pittsburgh, also in many other hospitals that I will tell you about later. Doctors gave me up and said there was no hope for me. Oh dear reader, this all came upon me through disobedience unto God, but He had mercy on me and knew that I had a soul. Luke 19:10, "For the Son of man is come to SEEK and to SAVE THAT WHICH WAS LOST." "O (sinner reader) thou that killest the prophets, and stonest them which are sent unto thee, how often would I have gathered thy children together, even as a hen gathereth her chickens under her wings, and YE WOULD NOT!"—Matthew 23:37.

If you be a sinner, as you read this testimony, has God been trying to talk to you through affliction? Have you had narrow escapes in wrecks and other close calls? Won't you please stop and let God talk to your heart if you have not already done so, and have not as yet found Jesus?

CHAPTER VI

The devil's love bug.

Maybe as some of you read this chapter you won't think so much of it, but I must expose to this younger generation and to the mothers and the fathers some of the snares and traps of the devil in order to warn them about their young girls especially. As a young man without God I started out on these new ventures at the age of about twenty. I was like the sailor you have heard about, who "has a girl in every port." The lust of the flesh of this younger generation, as you will agree with me, is one of the greatest enemies that God has today, and is the reason why so many hospitals are filled with our young girls and boys with these horrible diseases, not mentioning the names as you know them. My greatest weakness was running after young girls and young women and this is also the greatest weakness of the past generations and of today. But I thank God, there IS deliverance to give you victory over the lust of the flesh, and that victory is through JESUS. Jeremiah 32:27 says, "Behold I am the Lord, the God of all flesh: is there anything too hard for me?" The Word of God says in 2 Corinthians 6:14, "Be ye not unequally yoked together with unbelievers: for what fellowship hath righteousness with unrighteousness? and what communion hath light with darkness?" God does not want us to be unequally yoked together, and if you will trust God and obey Him, He will find you the right mate and be equally yoked together, and your marriage will then be the holy and blessed estate that God intended it should be. It is God's will to have both husband and wife saved and sanctified and to be ready for Heaven as their eternal Home.

I have been married but once, but am ashamed to mention some of the things that I did while in sin, but was not unlike the sinners of the younger generation and all the unmentionable sins they commit against one another, the purity of that virgin girl and pure boy being wrecked through the wiles of the devil. I Peter 5:8 says, "Be sober, be vigilant; because your adversary THE DEVIL, AS A ROARING LION, walketh about, SEEKING WHOM HE MAY DEVOUR."

May God help you to turn to this Cure and that is JESUS, and only through the Blood will you ever be able to defeat the devil and his works. Revelation 12:11, "And they overcame him (the devil) by the Blood of the Lamb, and by the Word of their testimony; and they loved not their lives unto the death." Please, mother and father, boy and girl, think about your generation to follow and your own soul in the end. Jesus is the only one who can solve the problem so that you may have happiness, joy and peace for home, family, the nation and for time and eternity. Jesus Christ is the ONLY CONQUEROR.

CHAPTER VII

I stayed in carnival life until I met a Cherokee Indian girl in Vinita, Oklahoma; who became my one and only wife.

Friends, this chapter is a little bit out of the ordinary, I had been all over the lands in 40 states and had met blondes, brunettes, red-heads, black-heads and all nationalities, and had promised to marry them, and also many other things and gave them nothing, as most of this younger generation do in like manner, except to please the lust of the flesh which is the most damnable thing this side of hell. I Peter 2:11 says, "Dearly beloved, I beseech you as strangers and pilgrims, abstain from FLESHLY LUSTS, WHICH WAR AGAINST THE SOUL." I John 2:15, 16 and 17 says, "Love not the world, neither the things that are in the world; If any man love the world, the love of the Father is not in him. For all that is in the world, the LUST OF THE FLESH, AND THE LUST OF THE EYES, AND THE PRIDE OF LIFE, is not of the Father, but is of the world. And the world passeth away, and the lust thereof: but he that doeth the will of God abideth for ever."

I drifted down into Vinita, Oklahoma in 1932 and became a dope fiend, pick pocket, and short changer—in other words, I was known as "The Duke of the Midway." You ought to have seen me, with my spats on, and I thought I was IT! With my

little pair of spats, and all fixed up I was so proud
I stunk, and you could almost smell me coming.
All this pride is born in the human heart, in my
heart and in your heart, and only Jesus can cleanse
it out. I John 2:16, " . . . and the PRIDE OF
LIFE, is not of the Father, but is of the world (or
the devil)." One of the three temptations and perhaps the greatest the devil put before Jesus Christ
the Son of God in the wilderness, was the tempta-
tion to PRIDE OF LIFE, Matthew 4:8, 9, 10.
But Jesus overcame Satan by his reply, "Then saith
Jesus unto him, Get thee hence Satan: for it is
written, Thou shalt worship the Lord thy God, and
him only shalt thou serve. Then the devil leav-
eth Him, and behold angels came and ministered
unto Him."

Dear reader, you cannot help yourself, but I am
doing my best to testify to the remedy and to the
mercies of God, and how He saved me from all
this sin and wretchedness, of dope, marihuanna, alcohol and all the curse that goes with it. So here
I was in 1932 with a carnival in Vinita, Oklahoma,
back of a gambling stand and this place is where
and how I met my one and only wife. Walking down
the Midway were two good looking, high-stepping,
full blooded Cherokee Indian girls. They had on ear
rings, dog chains, and strutting as proud as peacocks.
Don't you think I have not been there!! The
devil's love-bug began to work, and I said to myself, "Here she comes!" "Look at those little dresses."
The devil can beautify anything. Just put some
perfume on them and dress them up like the world.
To there I was back of my gambling joint, all lit

up on morphine and ensnared by other habits. So as they walked by the gambling stand, I said, "Hey girls!" and they stopped and looked over, and I said, "It must be recess in heaven. All the angels are down here." Also I said, "I hope you get your little wings clipped so you cannot fly back." So they stopped and I said, "Girls, the boss said to give all the good looking girls a free prize that came to the Fair, and you have one coming," so they walked over to the gambling stand, and I made up my mind to get the good looking one that had the long black hair rolled up on the back of her head like two biscuits. The Love-bug of the devil had a hook in my jaw and I know as you listen on down through this experience that you will see that this girl was not meant for me through God talking to my conscience.

After I kidded them a while, and turned my gambling wheel around for fun, showed them some of the devil's five and ten cent jewelry, showed them kewpie dolls, and asked them which one they wanted —the doll with the red dress, or the one with the blue dress,—I gave them both one, then I asked them how they and their husbands were getting along. Then the two sisters said they didn't have any husbands, and I said, "Goody, no husband."

I fell for the one named Helen, and asked her for a date that night. That was Thursday night of the week. She said, "O. K., meet me at eleven o'clock at the Cook House." I talked to them for a few minutes longer, and then went on down the Midway.

Helen Herrod met me at the Cook House and

we started to her home. May I mention the fact here that the mother of these girls could hardly speak English, although the girls themselves were very good looking and were also very well educated. Now as this girl and I walked along toward her home, with the love bug after us, this younger generation knows the rest of the story. Now please do not take offense at this and get mad at me, because I was there myself just as you have been. We began to play hands, and by the time we got to her house, I had almost asked her to marry me. Then we reached her home and went in the gate and up onto the front porch, and there was love the first night as most folks do these days.   •

As the devil is on a rampage to wreck young people's lives with sin and shame, I kissed her good night, made another date for Friday night, and propositioned her to be my wife; stole her Saturday night, shipped her Sunday night and married her Monday night; and this is the way the devil has love affairs stream-lined for this generation; but thank God, if you will let Jesus find you and you belong to Him, you will not make such tragic mistakes in choosing a mate, but you will be equally yoked together and your marriage will be the holy, happy and blessed union that God ordained it should be. Ephesians 5:22, 25, 27 says, "Wives, submit yourselves unto your own husbands, as unto the Lord. Husbands, love your wives, even as Christ also loved the church, and gave Himself for it; That He might sanctify and cleanse it with the washing of water by the Word. That He might present it to Himself a glorious church, not having

spot, or wrinkle, or any such thing; but that it
should be holy and without blemish." If you are
saved by the Blood of Jesus, and sanctified by His
Holy Spirit, what a happy home you will have, but
oh, without Jesus, thousands of young married
couples of today and also in the past are having a
hell on earth in their homes instead of their home
being a bit of heaven, and where they can truly
say "Home Sweet Home."

Here are some things that took place between my
wife and I during the two years of our married
life. What I did not do, she did. She was a sinner
and I was a still worse sinner. She was dance floor
crazy and I had all these other things tied to me
that I have told you about. She was dabbling into
everything and so was I. I accused her, and she accused me. She was out with other men, and I was
out with other women; in other words, we had no
God, no Christ, no church, no Sunday School, just
two of the devil's sinners doing the devil's work. We
didn't seem to be able to improve ourselves nor our
condition and we got no help from within our own
selves. We were always arguing, and fighting, tear-
ing up our apartment, throwing pots and pans,
skillets and dishes. She was a wild cat and I was
a Tom cat; she a she-devil and me a he-devil, and
when they got tied together the fur flew! On
one occasion she fixed me up proper. With her
devil's painted-up finger nails, she scratched me up
and down through the face until I looked like a wild
cat had gotten hold of me. Anyway, this is just
a few things the devil can get you tangled up in.

After two years of living in "hell," she and I

separated. She went one way and I went the other, and as far as I know, only God knows if she is living today. I have not seen her, but if Jesus tarries and I live and if she is still living, I am looking for her now to tell her the story of Jesus. I want her to look at me today, and I want to testify to her that Jesus loves her the same as He loves me, and to do unto her as He has done unto me. Ephesians 4:32, "And be ye kind one to another, tender-hearted, forgiving one another, even as God for Christ's sake hath forgiven you." Luke 6:31, "And as ye would that men should do to you, do ye also to them likewise."

CHAPTER VIII

Be sure your sins will find you out.
You reap what you sow.

Now dear reader, from reading thus far in my story you will see what dabbling in sin leads to. I was led into doing all the little things the devil would have me do of the underworld and his followers; yet, some people think there is no harm in setting up Kitty cats. Fathers, mothers, boys and girls, PLEASE stay away from these devices of the devil as I have warned you before in this testimony. I will now tell you how the devil really launched me out into deep water.

In the year of 1934 I drifted on down into Oklahoma and got myself tangled up with some counterfeiters who had some counterfeit money, and I got in possession of a great deal of it and passed it. We may think we are pretty smart, but God will surely punish sin. Numbers 32:23, "But if ye will not do so, behold, ye have sinned against the Lord: and BE SURE YOUR SIN WILL FIND YOU OUT."

Now after passing a great deal of this money, I drifted over into Vinita, Oklahoma again and got me a hotel room. While I was lying in bed in the hotel room a knock came to the door. I was lit up with morphine and whiskey, so I raised up and said, "Come in." A peculiar stranger he was. My sins had found me out. This stranger said, "Are

33

you Po Po Thomas?" Anyway, he threwed his coat back and said, "I am looking for you and now I have you." A large man he was and he rushed over, throwed the handcuffs on me and began to tell me of his visit. He was a United States Deputy Marshall. He took me down to the County jail in Vinita and locked me in.

The next morning I woke up in jail, looking 75 years in the face for passing counterfeit money. Then some people say, "no harm in Kitty cats at carnivals." On top of that I was a dope addict, had all this disease on my body and ready to drop into hell. I could not get any dope nor whiskey to ease my pain from the habit, so here I was in the jaws of hell, but THANK GOD the Christ of Calvary was still by my side. Matthew 9:13, "For I am not come to call the righteous but sinners to repentance." John 12:47, "For I came not to judge the world, but to SAVE the world."

I did not know it then, but it seems that I was permitted to lead the life I did in order to show you readers and sinners of this world that whosoever would come unto Him, He would pardon, and there is all power in His Blood. Isaiah 55:7, "Let the wicked forsake his way, and the unrighteous man his thoughts: and let him return unto the Lord, and He will have mercy upon him; and to our God, for He will abundantly pardon." Exodus 12: 13, "And the Blood shall be to you for a token upon the houses where ye are: and when I see the BLOOD, I will pass over you." In this condition I was left behind those prison bars, an outcast, health wrecked, all those terrible habits upon me and looking 75 years in the face. Dear reader, you wonder why I write this book. It is because I want the world to know that there is a Jesus that loves and has power to save, sanctify and heal. THANK GOD, He is a specialist on habits such as I have told you about. Isaiah 45:22, "Look unto me, and BE YE SAVED, all the ends of the earth: for I am God, and there is none else."

As I sat in my cell, here comes a United States Marshall to take me out and bind me over to the Grand Jury under a $35,000 bond, and then back to the jail. All my carnival friends forsook me, the world forsook me, but JESUS WILL NEVER FORSAKE YOU. Hebrews 13:5, " . . . for He hath said, I will never leave thee, nor forsake thee." I stayed in that Vinita County jail for seventy-two days, suffering under the agony of habit of dope, whiskey and marihuanna and with all these diseases on my body.

I would like to add here something about my brother, the only one I had. About this same time, he was also a dope fiend and a car thief, a gambler and robber, and he was picked up in Louisville, Kentucky and throwed in the Jefferson County jail with fourteen car raps against him. He was looking many years in the face. The dope habit had such a hold on him also. Because he couldn't get any dope, the second week they found him hanging from a steam pipe with a blanket around his neck. So my brother hanged himself and was dead and buried a long time before I knew about it.

Now back to my testimony. I was taken out of the Vinita jail on Plea Day and pleaded "guilty." It was in the city of Tulsa, Oklahoma where I pleaded guilty, and I got fifteen months for counterfeiting, and although I had five charges against me, the Judge and the Prosecutor had mercy on me through God in heaven and I know that God spoke to them. That was one time that I was really scared when I stood before that Judge. Just how I got by with all of those habits on me, and all of those things I had done, and how God worked miraculously with that Judge, instead of giving me the limit, is only a miracle. He only gave me fifteen months on each charge, running concurrently and I know God had His hand on this case. **PRAISE HIS NAME.** Isaiah 55:9, 10, "For my thoughts are not your thoughts, neither are your ways my ways, saith the Lord. For as the heavens are higher than the earth, so are my ways higher than your ways, and my thoughts than your thoughts." From Tulsa, Oklahoma, I was brought back to Vinita, Oklahoma to wait to be transferred to Leavenworth, Kansas, United States Penitentiary.

CHAPTER IX

The United States Penitentiary
at Leavenworth, Kansas

Here comes the man from the United States Penitentiary to gather the prisoners from jail to jail. He came in the jail and put the handcuffs on about six of us prisoners. Many of the other prisoners had much time to do and so could go along with me. Sin did all this. Romans 6:21, 23, "What fruit had ye then in those things whereof ye are now ashamed? for the end of those things is death. For the wages of sin is death; but the gift of God is ETERNAL LIFE through Jesus Christ our Lord." James 1:13, 14, 15, "Let no man say when he is tempted, I am tempted of God: for God cannot be tempted with evil, neither tempteth He any man: but every man is tempted, when he is drawn away of his own lust and enticed. Then when lust hath conceived, it bringeth forth sin: and sin, when it is finished, bringeth forth death."

So off we go to the Leavenworth Penitentiary. We arrived there, checked in quarters, they gave us a G.I. hair cut and examined us for diseases. How I got by with this dope habit, I do not know. Although my body was wrecked from sin and I had to be in the hospital much of the time while there, still the Mighty Hand of God and His mercies followed me, and I lived to tell the story. Psalm 103:

37

17, "But the mercy of the Lord is from everlasting to everlasting upon them that fear him . . . ." Psalm 23:6, "Surely goodness and MERCY shall follow me all the days of my life . . . ." Psalm 130:7, " . . . with the Lord there is MERCY, and with Him is plenteous REDEMPTION." God touched my body and I shook off the habits for the time being. God was working with me but the devil had me bound so with sin that I was planning in my mind how to get even with the world when I got outside of the prison walls again. This is of the devil, that old get-even spirit of the carnal heart. Romans 12:17, 20, "Recompense to no man evil for evil. Provide things honest in the sight of all men. Therefore if thine enemy hunger, feed him; if he thirst, give him drink: for in so doing thou shalt heap coals of fire on his head."

After I had done six months of my fifteen months, God sent a good Christian woman to the penitentiary to see if she could find someone who did not have anyone to help them to get a parole. By talking with her and through God's mercy and help I was granted parole from the Leavenworth penitentiary after eight months of my fifteen months sentence. The day came when I was to be pardoned, and out I went to catch the train to my parole advisor in Little Rock, Arkansas. I am ashamed to say that as soon as I hit the free world, the old desire of those old habits of sin still had me bound and I drifted back to the old gang again. However, I managed to hold off until I arrived at Little Rock and reported to my parole advisor. I then broke my parole, went back to the old habits, and back to the carnival life.

Friends, I told that poor old Christian woman a lie, and the Government of the United States, and off to the devil's crew again to thieve, rob, pick more pockets, short change more people, and back to the underworld, with no God, no hope in the future except to duck and dodge the laws, the policemen, the FBI, the sheriffs and the law-enforcement agencies of the land. Disease also began creeping back on my body. Hosea 8:7, "For they have sown the wind, and they shall reap the whirlwind . . . ." Galatians 6:7, "Be not deceived; God is not mocked: for whatsoever a man soweth, THAT SHALL HE ALSO REAP."

CHAPTER X

Even though I was the chief of sinners,
God held out to me His hand.

I drifted up and down the lands for three years in carnivals and everything the devil would have me do. I had been in hospitals. God only knows how I lived to tell this experience. By this time I was beginning to get ragged, my hair growing down my neck, my shoes worn out, all my friends gone, except Jesus. Proverbs 18:24, ". . . and there is a friend that sticketh closer than a brother." Psalm 46:1, "God is our refuge and strength, a very present help in trouble." He was still by my side, His mighty hand of mercy upon me. Psalm 139: 10, "Even there shall thy hand lead me, and thy right hand shall hold me."

O reader, if you could only have seen me when I was picked up at that time and the condition I was in, then you would not have wondered why I want the world to know about Jesus. Isaiah 55:1, "Ho, everyone that thirsteth, come ye to the waters, and he that hath no money; come ye, buy, and eat; yea, come, buy wine and milk without money and without price."

After being picked up by police, they finger-printed me. Oh, I was a sick man! No morphine, no whiskey, no nothing but SIN and SHAME and a wrecked body. On top of all that they gave me a chain gang suit to wear, and gave me fifteen days for vagrancy on the city dump yard, but that is only fifteen days that I did not do.

On the third day, 1938, here comes the United States Deputy Marshall. He came back to the bars of the cell and said, "Hello Tommy Thomas, I have been looking for you for years. Now you are headed back to the United States penitentiary." He asked me a few questions, and had me put on my other clothes that were so ragged. The Marshall said to them, "Have him ready, I will be back shortly." I knew where I was going, back yonder behind the cold prison walls to be an outcast, forsaken and forgotten by the world, but Jesus was still there. Psalm 23:4, ". . . for thou art with me." Psalm 59:16, "But I will sing of thy power; yea, I will sing aloud of thy mercy in the morning: for thou hast been my defence and refuge in the day of my trouble." PRAISE HIS HOLY NAME.

In about two hours the Marshall returned, picked me up and ushered me off to the Atlanta United States Federal penitentiary. I checked back in prison as before, about the same routine as in Leavenworth, but oh, my body and the habits! I was a miserable wreck but God touched me again and I managed to smother the habits, and God was with me through the remainder to finish my fifteen months in Atlanta Federal prison.

After being released from the Atlanta Federal prison I started right back to my old habits and my old gang, because I had no Jesus, no home, no people, nothing but sin and a wrecked body.

CHAPTER XI

Horrors of the chain gang in the south.

This was one of my most horrible experiences. This chain gang is known as one of the toughest in the south. I got this time for being drunk and stealing. Only the hand of God could have spared me in the condition I was in, to do the work that I was made to do while on chain gangs.

While I was on this chain gang, my body was wracked with disease, as I have said before, and I had all the sinful habits, but God has many ways to punish sinners, for, "What ye sow, ye shall reap."

This place was the place where I had the chains around my ankles. My ankles were swollen because of dropsy, but that did not make any difference. I told the authorities I was sick with heart trouble and many other diseases, and they saw it for themselves. They told me I should never have come there, so just picture the punishment that I was suffering. On top of that, they would not get a doctor for me. The food was terrible; sleeping quarters terrible—bed-bugs and lice, filth—no inside rest rooms.

My dear friends, I pray that you will never come in contact with this horrible place. Many things I cannot express. Go to work of a morning around seven o'clock and work until five o'clock that evening, with the chains on your legs, the striped suit on, a shovel or pick in your hand and a guard standing over you with a sawed-off shot gun, bloodhounds tied on the hillside. Oh, such horrible punishment. Sin did it all. And these guards would curse you if you told them you were sick. I showed them my ankles, how they were swollen, and asked for a doctor, but they would say, "No doctor. Die and we will get you out of the way."

Reader, this is only one experience of many I have gone through in the Southland on chain gangs and in stockades. Why? all because I had no God. So my word to all is, "There is a Christ who is able to keep all from this horrible punishment and hell in the end." Praise His name!

CHAPTER XII

Hospital experience in Wilmington, North Carolina.

After wandering down in the southlands in the year of 1940, I was in Wilmington, North Carolina in a beer parlor. I have said before I had heart trouble and dropsy. I was standing at the bar—ragged, disgusted, trying to find pleasure and ease for my body—peace—by drinking the devil's slop, and suddenly a heart attack came upon me. To the floor I fell. The next thing I remembered I was in the emergency room in Wilmington Hospital. They asked me some questions. Oh, if you could only have seen me, you would say, Is it possible that God—that Stranger of Galilee, could heal a man in such condition?

The doctors took my record as my mind was clouded and foggy, and checked me in the emergency ward.

After God revived me, the doctors came around and after taking the examination, returned in a couple of days and shook their heads and said, "The sooner he dies, the better off he will be. So far as we are concerned, it is out of our hands. We have gone as far as we know how."

But, oh, dear reader, there is One who has all power to save, to heal, and to sanctify. Do you wonder why I love Him so?

Again He laid His hand upon me, touched my body, turned me out of the hospital, but I was so

44

ignorant—never had heard of Jesus Christ, never knew that it was God touching me, and that the Holy Ghost had His mighty hand upon me all the time. Oh, how I do love Him for His longsuffering, not willing that any should perish. Dear reader, I am just a pattern. Don't take the chance I did, to show the power of the touch of the sacred hand of God. At this very moment, if you be a sinner, may these words touch your heart. May you meet this Stranger, so that you will never be sorry through time and eternity.

CHAPTER XIII

A vision of Jesus on the Cross.

After wandering back in carnival life, in jails and out of jails, in hospitals and out of hospitals, only God's mercy has taken me through such experiences. I wandered up to Lorain, Ohio, October, 1942. There I wandered out on the Bowery, Lake Erie water front and drank bay rum, canned heat, and got drunk. There, with the rest of the bums, I passed out.

The next thing I remember, I awoke in Lorain City jail without my clothes. Someone even stole my pants. In the meantime, the other prisoners in the jail said I was talking in my sleep, but this was something that I actually saw. It was not a dream. I have never forgotten this because it was supernatural, from God. As the Bible says, Acts 2:17, ". . . your young men shall see visions and your old men shall dream dreams."

So when I came to, the men were telling me what I said. I am now telling you what I saw as I lay there on that bunk. It seemed as though I was glued to that bunk. There appeared to me Jesus on the cross—not nailed, just stuck there. Above His head was a halo and underneath the cross was a large knife, and it seemed as though this cross swung close to my neck. The prisoners said I was saying: "Oh, Jesus, don't cut my head off." He looked at me from the cross with that pleasant smile

46

and said, "Come unto Me, I have work for you to do."

I said, "Lord, where?"

This was the first time I realized that God was talking to me. Before this, I thought I was seeing things, but this time it was real. Praise His name! Oh God, if it be Thy will speak to people who are without Thee, through visions and dreams.

Dear reader, has God ever spoken to you like this? I warn you as a man who loves God and souls, you had better heed. This is more dangerous than fork-tongued lightning to try to run from God. But thank God, I did not run. That is why I am so happy. I began to realize that something supernatural was dealing with me, which is the Spirit of God, praise His name!

From there out of jail, I went to Mansfield, Ohio. Here I was in another jail and hospital, but thank God, He still had His hand on me, turned me out, started me down the highway, even though I was a wreck of sin, diseased body—not telling of many other experiences I had in hospitals and jails.

Please give your heart to God before some horrible tragedy befalls you is my plea, because there is power in the blood of Jesus.

CHAPTER XIV

Was sentenced eleven days for vagrancy at Marion,
Ohio. Thank God for Marion,
Ohio. county jail.

Wandering down the highway in November, 1942, a man picked me up and took me to Marion, Ohio. I was nervous. All this disease on my body, all these habits made me extremely nervous.

When I got into Marion, I wandered down to the pool hall with the devil's game. Why? Because they have no God. There, I became involved in drinking, playing pool all afternoon. I got into Marion about ten o'clock in the morning and played until about eleven o'clock that night. By that time, I was all lit up on wine, whiskey, and hopped up in the devil's hell hole. Oh, what a terrible sight I was. What a pool hustler. So I wandered out of the pool room and beer parlor to the Pennsylvania Railroad Station in Marion. I sat down, fell off to sleep with a half pint of wine in my pocket. But the Bible says, "Be sure your sin will find you out." About one thirty in the morning of November, 1942, a man walked up to me and shook me by the arm, saying, "What are you doing here?" He appeared to be a railroad detective. He said: "Why aren't you working? Why aren't you in the army?" He searched me and found the wine on me. I told him I was sick, showed him my feet how they were swollen from dropsy and that I had heart trouble, and pellagra. I also told him that I had been in two Federal prisons. So he said, "Come with me, I have a place for a man like you." So, to the jail he took me.

That night, as I was full of beer and whiskey and wine, I didn't know what I was talking about to a certain extent, but Jesus was still with me.

They threw me in a cell and I went to sleep. But, oh, the next morning, the terrible after effects of this terrible drinking! And I was forsaken and forgotten behind those prison bars. No doctor to settle my nerves. No God and ready to drop in hell, but the Holy Ghost was talking to me, saying, "What if you would die, where would you go?"

Oh, what a horrible experience this was! I walked the cell and wrung my hands. I didn't know how to pray. Nobody had ever told me about Jesus. I thank God that He let me experience this, that I might warn others never to sin as I have. Oh, how I do love Him for His mercy! Friend, if you are not saved, have you ever been in close quarters when something would tell your conscience, "What would you do if you were to die without God?" This is the Spirit of Almighty God.

Here I was in this condition. About nine o'clock in the morning, they came for me to take me for trial. They questioned me and fingerprinted me. I was used to this as I have such records all over the country, but, oh, the terrible record was my record that God had against me.

Then they took me before the judge. The judge looked at me and asked me if I was guilty of vagrancy, and gave me eleven days in the Marion

County jail. That's one eleven days that I am proud the judge gave me. I will never regret those days.

Then they rushed me over to the county jail, took my name and put me in jail. So there I was another time, paying for sin I had committed.

I explained to the jailer my condition. I had the doctor. If I remember right, I think that I had a heart attack while in Marion County jail, as I cannot remember everything just exactly, but there was one thing that happened there that will stand while the world's on fire, by God's help! The Blood of Jesus and the way of Holiness, as you will hear a little later on.

I stayed in jail about four days and some church workers came in. You saw the man's picture, Rev. Howard Hughes, who led me to God. He was a man of God, a Christian of the Baptist denomination.

This was the first service he had held in this jail while I was there, but the devil had me bound so with sin and its habits, and my body was so wrecked with disease, it seemed as though all hope was gone and I would not come out at this time and listen to the service. But, the power that is in the Blood of Jesus no human tongue can tell. He is all power.

This was the first jail service I had ever heard. I would not come out to listen to the songs of Zion and the preaching of God's Word. Brother Hughes had other Christians with him, especially a little girl who played an accordion. They were always passing out tracts before this jail service. I had been reading tracts about Jesus that I had found in the jail blocks. These tracts had me in such a condition of conviction that I could not eat, sleep, afraid to go to sleep, afraid I'd die. This was the Spirit of God talking to my heart. Oh, how I walked those cells. And the perspiration—I was sweating like a colored man at an election. I mean the Holy Ghost had me in a tail spin, but thank God for praying saints of Israel who have never ceased praying for lost men, and forsaken boys back of the cold prison bars. Since my conversion I carry a mighty burden for that class and for all the world.

Brother Hughes and his workers went ahead with their services. This was in December. Left the jail between this time and Christmas day. Talk about a man being under old-time Sinai conviction, I was. Somebody had hold of God for my soul, and I believe that my grandmother on my Dad's side was the cause of my conversion by her prayers, and a man like Brother Hughes. I give God all the glory!

CHAPTER XV

My conversion on Christmas Day, 1942, in Marion County Jail.

Thank God for men and women whom He can use.

Brother Hughes and the little girl that I told you about in the previous chapter, Pauline Kidd, who played the accordion, came back with other workers to the jail on Christmas Day. It seemed as though a peculiar atmosphere came upon that jail that day. While they were on the outside waiting, the jailer yelled through the port hole, "Boys, we have a treat for you this Christmas Day. We are going to have Brother Hughes and the singers for a jail service." This time, my heart was glad. The Holy Spirit of God had softened my heart, like old Pharaoh's, through some saint's prayers.

So they pulled the benches up and we formed a circle, about fifteen of us. This time, I walked out just as calm, but during the time between the service that Brother Hughes held the first time and this, God had really been talking to me.

A lot of people do not believe in tracts. As this book is being written, I still have the tract, which, as far as I know, helped lead me to God. The name of the tract is, "Eternity, Where Will You Spend It?" Someone prayed down conviction on my soul as I read this tract and many others.

In came the Christian workers. I can see Brother

Hughes now with tears running down his cheeks—
that man of God, filled with the love of God,
with the charm of an angel on his face, and the
other Christians, and this young girl with her accordion with the smile of an angel. Oh, I thought
these were the most beautiful people I ever saw,
and they were at that time.

So as I sat on that bench on Christmas Day, 1942,
about three thirty in the afternoon, to experience
something that all should experience, that the world
cannot give nor take away.

The first thing taking place in this religious service was they sang a gospel hymn and it got hold of
me. The Holy Ghost had hold of me, which is the
Spirit of God. Then they prayed, and I began to
get under conviction. Then after prayer, this young
girl, Pauline Kidd, if I remember, sang a song, or a
song was sung and God broke me up. This song
was, "What A Friend We Have In Jesus." I knew
then I was ready for the altar, but this little man
of God, Brother Hughes, had some of the other
people to testify, especially one man who had been
saved in the past in this same jail. Then he took
his Bible, turned to the simple words of God about
His Son, the blood and the power that could save,
heal and sanctify a soul like me, *and your soul* likewise.

Brother Hughes seemed to be pointing his finger
right at me, with tears running down his cheeks
and saying, "Jesus can save you," and after a few
minutes preaching, God was on the scene. As near
as I can remember, we all bowed our heads to pray
and in the meantime, I got up and went back to

my cell, by the old bunk where God and I had been wrestling for about seven days. Finally, I went to my knees, and the service in the front was dismissed, as far as I knew, and Brother Hughes and the other Christians left, so what time it was, I do not know, but I know I was on my knees praying there in that jail, and I was behind those bars on Christmas Day—not a friend in the world except that Friend who is a Friend to all, Jesus, the Stranger of Galilee, saying, "Come unto me, all ye that labor and are heavy laden and I will give you rest." That wee voice talking into my ear and heart.

I said from my heart, "Jesus, what would Thou have me do?" And it felt as though the devil's imps were there with pitch forks, trying to fork me into hell, but Jesus said, "Pay them no mind, I have the power to overcome death, hell and judgment."

Oh, as the memories wracked my brain about the things I had done in the past, how I had robbed people, and so on, the devil said, "How will you ever straighten these things out?"

But, oh, a voice much stronger than this voice of the devil spoke to Tommy's heart, "Do you believe me?" But about that time, I said, "You did unto others and I do believe you can forgive me for all the evil I have done. You said in your Word that your grace is sufficient. You will help me to make all things right. Oh, I want peace and happiness. I have been seeking up and down the land for about thirty years in forty states."

As I said before in the beginning of this book—carnivals, hell holes, beer, whiskey, habits, night clubs and all the rest of the devil's field, I searched, but never found any peace. But on that Christmas Day, 1942, behind prison bars, I found that peace between five and six o'clock. And now I can say when I said yes to Jesus, "Goodby, old world, I'm through," and Jesus came into my life, and "behold, old things passed away and behold all things became new." Then to tell the greatest of all, what a happy man I am today.

I used to faint all the time. I have not fainted one time since that Christmas Day, 1942. Pellagra has gone from my body, dropsy, first stage of a cancer, only by the touch of the Sacred Hand of Almighty God. Does God still perform miracles today?

That very day I began teaching and preaching about the power of the Blood of Jesus and His power to heal. So the jailer, his wife and the sheriff saw such a change in my life, my actions and my ways, such a smile upon my face, as they said. I only had two or three days to go until my sentence would be up, so they said, "Loose him and let him go." The jailer and his wife saw such a change in me; they helped me get a start and get a job at the Harding Hotel, and also attended church with me after that. So I am just Believing Tommy Thomas in God, an old sinner saved by Grace, by the Blood and the way of Holiness.

Won't you, dear reader, if you do not know this wonderful Christ, let this book of testimony about the supernatural, dynamic powers of God, speak to your heart from the Spirit, that you, too, can be as happy as I am, and all of God's people while on this earth, and oh, what about spending eternity with Jesus and the streets of gold, the saints of God; happiness, joy and peace for time and eternity—my prayer for all, if I never see you on this earth, is that I will meet you in heaven through this testimony, by the Blood of Jesus Christ, and the way of Second Blessing Holiness.

Reader of this book, may I tell you this? If what I have got—which is old time salvation—is not better than carnival life, circus life, bowling alleys, night clubs, roller rinks, ball games, hell holes and taverns, lust and the attractions of worldly pleasures, I would go back where I came from. But, thank God, I say hurray for Jesus. I have what every heart longs for; peace, joy and happiness that nothing can disturb.

As you have read what God has done with this boy—Tommy Thomas, the impossible, that the world, doctors, hospitals, medicine, chain gangs, Keeley cures, penitentiaries and jails could not do, but all things are possible with God to them that believe; if you be, dear reader, in the shape that I was before Jesus found me, won't you please just give Jesus one chance at your heart and life? You will never be sorry throughout time and eternity.

This world of sinners are drinking from the pleasures of the world such as beer mugs, whiskey glasses, trying to satisfy that thirst to that heart and life, but they only find this by doing these things to partake of the beer mugs, whiskey glasses and eventually lose their souls, if they fail to find this Christ.

But now I say—and I am not drinking from the beer mugs or whiskey glasses or seeking pleasure from this entertainment world, but I say that I and all God's people are drinking from the Fountain that never runs dry. I have an over-flowing well from the Fountain of Water of Life. I say hurray for Jesus. Try Him one time—Jesus.

CHAPTER XVI

Experience through faith in God since my conversion

After staying in Marion over three months, I went out amongst my carnival friends, preaching the Gospel as a war bond salesman and fund organizer, the army having rejected me because of my record. Needless to say, this was all worked out by God. Many of my carnival friends believed me. Many times I prayed with them in their trailers. They cried and wept but it seems as though they are a people who are hard to reach. Reader, if you be a saint of God, pray for my carnival friends. There are multitudes of them who don't even know there is a God.

After six months telling them of Jesus and they saw what a change in me there was, they could hardly believe—but they knew it was supernatural, not from man, but of God. I left my testimony with them and traveled down to Gulfport, Miss., and there for the first time, I heard of Second Blessing Holiness, when I became affiliated with the Nazarenes, Pilgrims, Wesleyans, and all people who preach and live Second Blessing Holiness.

CHAPTER XVII

The battle I had getting Second Blessing Holiness.

For about eighteen months, I battled with inbred sin, which is known as carnality. But the good I accomplished came through working and seeking, following the Nazarenes, Pilgrims and Wesleyan camp meetings until 1945, at a camp meeting at Santown, Delaware I found Second Blessing Holiness at one-thirty in the morning. I have been having the time of my life ever since. I say Hurray for Jesus and the way of Holiness.

You who read this book, who are saved but not sanctified, just keep seeking, pay the price and I'll assure you that you will eventually find this way, which means just a little heaven here. Be waiting to enter big Heaven. I say Glory!

Now that I have had my breakfast and dinner at God's table, I am now waiting for the Marriage Supper of the Lamb. You may have eaten delicious meals, but you forget all about them. But here are two meals at God's table you will never forget. Saved by the blood of Jesus which is breakfast. Sanctified by the Holy Ghost—that is dinner—what a meal! Look who prepared them, Jesus. Even the angels serve them. I say Hurray for God's table and food. The table is always ready—one price to all—your sins is the price for your first meal, breakfast, and for your dinner, forsake all, tell the world goodby. Then you will be feasting on Holiness at God's table. Not only here, but oh, waiting for the Marriage Supper of the Lamb, and only those who have paid for breakfast and dinner will partake in the Marriage Supper of the Lamb. Are you ready? Thank God, you can be if you will only obey that small voice which says you "ought to be saved, reclaimed and sanctified." Your conscience is the umpire of God. This is how the Spirit speaks to you. It is more dangerous than forked tongue lightning to disobey the voice of God. Please surrender now if you are not ready to meet God.

I am in the soul business for my Jesus. That is my aim, so I believe, working for Him giving God all the glory and praise. I have now a special evangelistic line with the Pilgrim Holiness denomination, but work with the Nazarenes and Wesleyans, or any denomination that preaches and believes in Second Blessing Holiness.

I am just a child of the King. God has given me while writing this book in my last seven revivals, about 1,400 seekers at the altar, many finding God and finding holiness. Praise His name, there is all power in the name of Jesus, the Blood and the Holy Ghost.

I am just journeying through on my way to Heaven. Won't you join me? It is wonderful, wonderful, what the Lord has done. He can do the same for you. "Whosoever will" means all classes.

This book, a testimony sent out into the world to bless others, from a happy little man of God.

CHAPTER XVIII

God has his hands on the waterspout.

I am not Elijah, but I am one of his running mates.

I will give this testimony to show you God answers prayer. I am giving this testimony to show how big God is, and what kind of power He has.

I was having a street meeting. It was raining. This is why they call me Believing Thomas.

As we went to the corner, it was raining hard, so I got on my knees with my other workers, and said, "God, if you will stop this rain, I will testify."

Within three minutes it stopped raining and when we got on the corner with the drums, we sang a song and the people were astonished at how this rain was stopped so quickly.

I testified and what a meeting we had for about forty-five minutes.

We went back to the church and the rain started again. If you believe Him, God has supernatural power.

Give Him the glory, not me.

CHAPTER XIX

God answers prayer for car.

I give this testimony for the glory of God, and only God could have done this.

I had a Model A Ford that God gave me. I was in a revival in North Carolina.

I have much baggage and loud speakers and I needed a larger car, so I began to pray. God showed me a car with red wheels.

Although I had a good Model A, it was too small as I do much traveling, and as a rule I have lots of tracts in my car. So I found the car with the red wheels. It cost $1100 and my Ford. The man I bought it from was an ex-soldier of World War II. The car was in excellent shape, but I only had $3.00 in my pocket.

This happened in October, 1946. So I began to pray. I said: "God, you know who's got the $1100.00," and the next morning, the pastor of the Nazarene Church, Ralph Sexton—I went to him and talked to him. He said, "Let's go."

We got into his car, drove four miles out of town to a saint of God named Miss Vonnie K. Bell, Route 3, Asheville, North Carolina, as she had a little money and always helped God's people.

So we went to her, talked to her, had prayer. She went to the bank, and here was another miracle!

God is big, only believe Him.

Miss Bell gave me $1,000. Told me to just pay as I saw fit. I told her I would pay her $50.00 a month. She said, "Anyway, I'll trust the good Lord because I know you are a man of God."

I am now driving that 1941 Chevrolet coupe while writing this book for the glory of God, telling the name-fame and the power of God, from house to house, from door to door, from town to town and from shore to shore.

Oh, never doubt God, just believe. Give Him the glory.

And in this revival, God gave the Nazarene Church in Asheville, better than 400 seekers. Praise His name.

CHAPTER XX

This is a prophecy inspired by the Holy Ghost.

I have many others. I will tell this one.

I was in a revival in North Carolina. God showed me caskets for three days. I kept saying from the pulpit that tragedy would follow this revival. The last night I was burdened, my heart was heavy. I told the people, and here is what happened.

On Monday morning after the revival closed, a man two doors below the tent meeting went out to get in his car, took hold of the door handle and dropped dead. I still have the letter received from the pastor, telling me about it, after I left that community. I also have many other letters, telling where I have prophesied and where terrible things happened after every revival I have been in.

The worst tragedy of all, I think, this man was without God. Think, reader, think. This could have been you. If you are without God please prepare to meet your God before it is too late.

As I was holding a revival in Thomasville, North Carolina, 1946, I was praying in the church basement. God showed me a terrible tragedy. I told it from the pulpit that morning, so after church, at the house of the pastor, Rev. Cockman of the Pilgrim Holiness Church, as had been advertised, there were great motorcycle races on the other side of the town. As the motorcycles went by about one o'clock, I told the pastor and his family, "I feel so peculiar, something is going to happen this afternoon." I thought, will it be someone without God, as the cars and motorcycles went by, seeking pleasure of the world on the Sabbath day. This is a warning to people to keep God's Sabbath Day holy. As the race went on at the track, those people around the track looked on as the drivers were speeding away , when suddenly one motorcycle got out of control and went through the crowd. In about ten minutes three ambulances rushed down the street toward the tragedy, and one woman's brains were knocked out and nine other people were broken up, skinned up and carried to the hospital. So far as we know, this poor woman went out to meet God unprepared.

Please keep God's Sabbath Day holy. Go to church and Sunday School. Job 36:18, ". . . beware lest he take thee away with his stroke: then a great ransom cannot deliver thee." Too late! There is no chance for the Blood to reach you after breath leaves this body.

May God help us, is my prayer.

CHAPTER XXI

God, who closed the lions' mouths,
closed a dog's mouth.

While in a street meeting in Indiana I was preaching away about the atomic bombs of God, 2 Peter, third chapter. The crowd was snickering and laughing.

All at once a dog came bounding out of the alley with his bristles all raised, and barking, ran up close to me, like he was going to bite me, and the words came to my mind that Daniel was saved from the lion's mouth. I knew that God had power to close the pooch's mouth, so I pointed my finger at the dog and said these words, "I rebuke you in the name of Jesus Christ," and the dog ran down the street, like it was a bolt of lightning. People were astonished, and that was the end of the laughing and the dog on the street corner. And the people told one another of that little man who rebuked the dog on the street corner. What a revival followed!

God still lives, give God the glory and the praise, always. This was supernatural, dynamic power from God. I say hurray for Jesus.

Readers, I could tell of miracle after miracle. God has miraculously answered prayer, such as that of Daniel in the lions' den, the Hebrew children, Peter, Paul, James, John, Moody, Finney and Wesley, and all others from generation to generation. And He is still anxious today to answer prayer if you will not doubt.

66

CHAPTER XXII

God also stops babies from crying
in service of a revival.

Many times during our revivals the devil fights me much with all the things that he can, such as sending bats in the church. I also rebuked them in the name of Jesus and out they went. This has happened many times, as you will learn if you happen to contact people who have been where I preached in revivals. Babies have been crying. not only one but many of them. I have said these words, "Lord, Thou knowest the little baby cannot help itself, because he is born with the devil in him, but Lord, you have power over the devil, hell, sin and the judgment. Please, if it be Thy will, rebuke these babies in the name of Jesus. It will help me to get people to the altar by showing them through me, who is a vessel meet for the Master's use, as Philip and Daniel were. Please grant this prayer, close these babies' mouths for Jesus' sake." This He did. Give Him the glory.

That is why God helps me to bring people from sin and darkness to light and glory. That is what this world is looking for, supernatural power.

With these miracles, I will close these testimonies. I could write on and on, but these are just a few to let you know that God is the power of powers, and the God of gods. Bring all to Him. Glorify Him. •I am praising His name.

CHAPTER XXIII

Take heed to this warning.

Dear reader, this book is a testimony to expound the powers of the Blood of Jesus and the way of Holiness and what happens. This same Jesus can bring salvation to whosoever will for time and eternity, but on the other hand, remember, there is for all who will not repent, a lake of God's boiling wrath of brimstone and fire forever and ever.

Please, if you be without God, don't take this chance which I have taken. People say they don't love Tojo, Hitler, Mussolini, Japan and Germany and others of their characters; hypocrites and professors, so I warn you please, to shun hell, which is God's penitentiary for all nations and people who forget God. This place will be thickly populated with such characters. Please escape by repenting of your sins now, tomorrow may be too late.

CHAPTER XXIV

A sketch of my life.

I will say this in a way that you will understand.

You know, God loves a little spiritual morale. He made monkeys and parrots and He made me. He surely must. I used to be a clown for the devil, but now I am an acrobat for the Lord. Also a thief and robber for Jesus, stealing souls for His Kingdom, snatching them out of the burning, by the Blood and the Way of Holiness.

If I am still living, all who read this book, and you hear of a revival near by where I am in a tabernacle, church or auditorium in a near-by city, come around and I will convince you that I am an acrobat for the Lord.

Many people tell me that I am crazy. They tell the truth. I am crazy for the Lord but I do not know who they are crazy for. I have been in forty states while writing this book. Thank God, I haven't made an insane asylum yet.

I was born at Cookeville, Putnam County, Tenn. Moved to West Virginia at the age of eight, to the town known as Williamson, in Bloody Mingo County, West Virginia. This is the county of the Hatfield-McCoy feud in the hills of West Virginia. Thank God, I don't handle any snakes and I preach and teach and pray in English. I say hurray for Second Blessing Holiness.

I will use my by-word: "AIN'T I A SIGHT ON THE DEVIL?" If you will meet me in person, I will convince you with the help of the Holy Ghost that I am a mystery to the world and a puzzle to the devil. Amen!

CPSIA information can be obtained
at www.ICGtesting.com
Printed in the USA
BVHW031127060321
601818BV00019B/316